MW00989661

®

SIGN LANGUAGE

D!RTY ®

SIGN LANGUAGE

Everyday Slang from "What's Up?" to "F*%# Off!"

ALLISON O & VAN JAMES T

*signs illustrated by **EVAN WONDOLOWSKI***
*artwork illustrated by **LINDSAY MACK***

Ulysses Press

Text Copyright © 2011 Allison O and Van James T. Design and concept © 2011 Ulysses Press and its licensors. Sign illustrations © 2011 Evan Wondolowski. All other illustrations © 2011 Lindsay Mack. All rights reserved, including the right to reproduce this book or portions thereof in any form whatsoever, except for use by a reviewer in connection with a review.

Published by:
Ulysses Press
P.O. Box 3440
Berkeley, CA 94703
www.ulyssespress.com

ISBN: 978-1-56975-786-4
Library of Congress Control Number: 2011926012

Printed in Canada by Webcom

10 9 8 7 6 5 4 3

Acquisitions editor: Keith Riegert
Managing editor: Claire Chun
Production: Abigail Reser
Proofreader: Lauren Harrison
Interior design: what!design @ whatweb.com
Cover design: Double R Design
Front cover photo: Beethoven © HultonArchive/istockphoto.com; woman © LUGO/istockphoto.com
Back cover color illustration: Lindsay Mack

Distributed by Publishers Group West

Ulysses Press holds a federally registered trademark for the Dirty series Reg. No. 3,928,097.

*With much love to those who are deaf-blind and
all those who have ever had anyone doubt their
intelligence just because of the language they speak.*

TABLE OF CONTENTS

•••••Acknowledgments

We'd like to thank Ryan Barrett (collaborative contributor), Amy Dignan, Angela Villareal, Camille Moreno, Kelli Wright, Lynn Jablonski, Malinda Tran, Michelle Albrecht, Michelle Kartheiser, Ruby Doerr, Sean Norman, Seth Farlin, Stephanie Uhren and many more...

USING THIS BOOK

This book was written with the assumption that you already have a good handle on sign language. If you failed to get the gist from the cover, this is a slang book, and the following pages won't show you how to quickly sign "Where is the train station?" or "My name is Chad, what's yours?" Chances are, you've learned quite a bit of sign language but nobody's bothered to teach you how to tell the douchebag at the bar to "fuck off," or how to inform your friend that his dick is abnormally small. If that's just the book you've been looking for, you've found it! We're about to school you on the most some useful words, phrases and curses that Thomas Gallaudet only wished he knew.

You might be wondering if this book covers all sign language dialects. While we've tried to gather the most common sign slang from around the country, we'll be the first to admit that this guide has distinctly Chicago accent to it. Why? Because Chicago is awesome—it's a huge, international city that revolutionized pizza and mobsters like New York never could—and packs a trendy, diverse community of hard-of-hearing people. It's also where we live.

Unlike common foreign languages like Spanish, Mandarin or Luxembourgish, there's really no universal form of sign language. The phrases and signs not only change from state to state, but city to city. So don't be surprised if some of the terms in this book get you a laugh, get you laid or get you a punch in the face, and others just get you a blank stare and a "lost in translation" shrug. Just keep signing. After all, while there's no better way to learn sign language than total immersion in a deaf community, *Dirty Sign Language* is a great place to develop the confidence to tell your new deaf friends that they "fucking rock."

So what are you waiting for? Go get your dirty on!

·····Simple tips on signing

Wanna sign like a pro? Here are some basic tips to hold the attention of the people you're signing to. Maintain eye contact so that it's apparent who you're chatting up; this also gives the recipient a clearer view of your lips (for lip-reading, of course). Speak while you sign; many deaf people also read lips, and when you're a beginning signer, your deaf friends may be relying more on what you say than what you sign. Be sure you have enough space so you can freely move your arms and really get into the conversation without knocking things over. Be free with your emotions and really let them show; using facial expressions helps you get across the tone of what you're saying when someone can't hear your voice change in volume, pitch and cadence. Sit or stand face to face; signing is easier to understand when you are face to face than side to side. And finally, if you're a beginner, take your time and sign clearly so your signs don't blend together and become confusing.

All right, some of the basic rules may not work in practice. Like if you're biking or kayaking, how the hell are you going to sit face to face? Just be sure you sign away from your body

MIX AND MATCH)))

This book is full of simple phrases that you can match up with different sentence endings so you can express yourself any way you want. When you see the beginning of a phrase that ends with ellipses, it's followed by a few options of how you would complete the sentence.

For example, "I wanna..." might be followed by "...sleep," "eat," or "fuck." With a few basics under your belt, you'll never be at a loss for signs.

so you don't block the view. Also keep it brief and concise; for God's sake, you're not gonna hold a debate on religion, politics or what the best TV show is unless you stop to talk.

But the best way to get better and increase your vocabulary is to hang out with deaf people. So go party, have a pint, converse at lunch or play sports with a deaf person, or if you're lucky, pick up a hot deafie and learn all the best dirty words while you do them!

THE ALPHABET

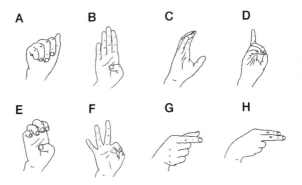

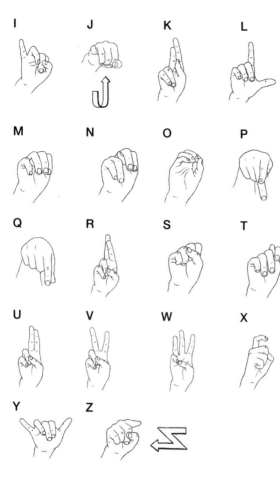

I J K L

M N O P

Q R S T

U V W X

Y Z

NUMBERS

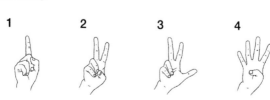

1 2 3 4

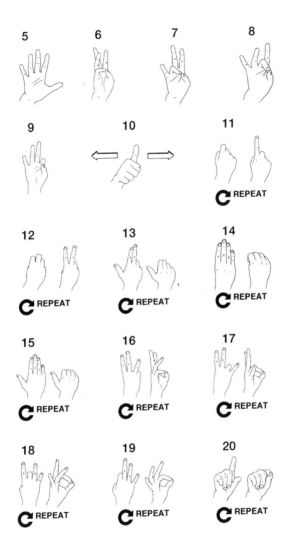

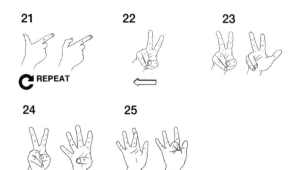

CHAPTER 1

HOWDY
SIGN LANGUAGE

Looking to start things off on the right foot with that cute deaf girl across the room? First off, don't be the dumbass who throws something at her to get her attention—that's just rude. Instead, gently tap her on the shoulder, or wave in her direction.

Once you're talking, be yourself! You don't need to be more polite or "sensitive" just because you're signing. If you swear when you're speaking out loud, do the same with your signs. Don't clean up your language or dumb it down; it's insulting to think just because someone is deaf they can't take it.

·····Hello

Hi

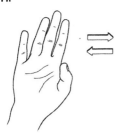

Howdy

Good mornin'

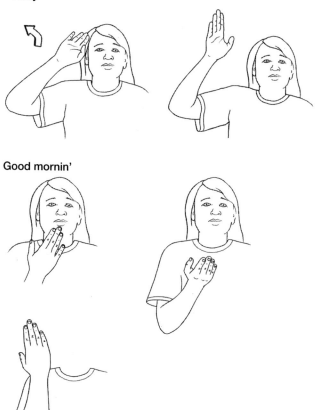

Afternoon

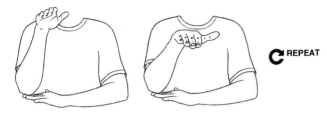

REPEAT

G'night

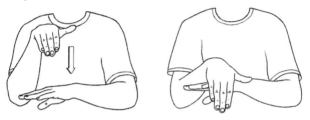

What's up...?

What up...? (laid-back sign for "What's up?")

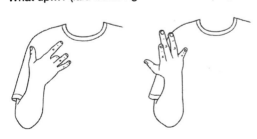

dude

Some words don't have signs, or you may not know them; then you just spell it out.

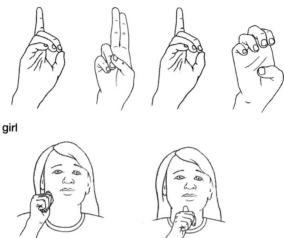

girl

my deafies

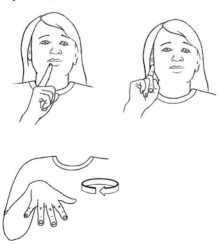

What's new?

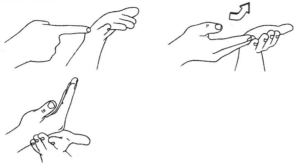

Eh, same old, same old.

REPEAT

Not much.

Shit if I know.

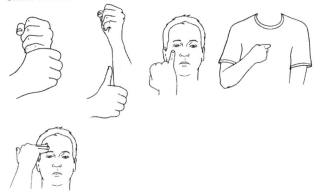

How you been?

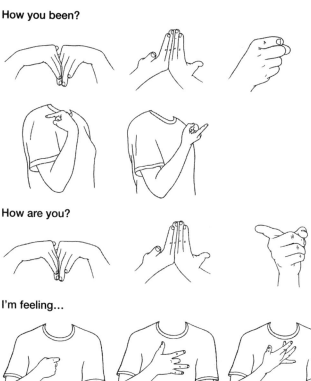

How are you?

I'm feeling…

crappy.

↻ REPEAT

stressed.

C REPEAT

happy.

C REPEAT 2X

great!

pissed off.

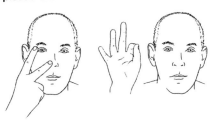

Nice to meet you.

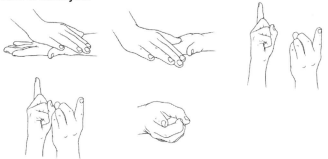

▪▪▪▪▪It's all in the name

Saying someone's name in sign language can be far more interesting than the way you'd write it. This is because there is no one way to say a name. For simple impersonal signs, use the first letter of the name and place it outward from the face (forehead for masculine, jaw for feminine).

However, more personal name signs tend to incorporate elements of the person's appearance or personality. A guy named Sean who has attention deficit disorder may be an "S" bouncing on the opposite palm—translated as "Hyper-as-Shit Sean."

What's your name again?

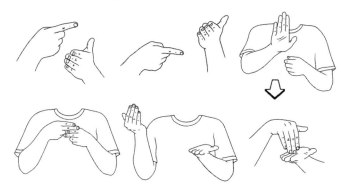

Wanna grab a drink?

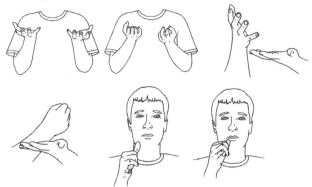

Want to see a movie?

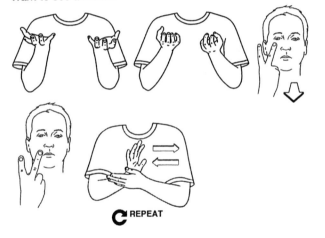

C REPEAT

·····Thank you

Thanks.

You rock!

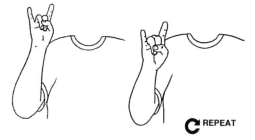

↻ REPEAT

You're welcome.

No prob!

  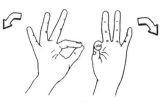

REPEAT

Forget about it.

Please.

Please could I text you sometime?

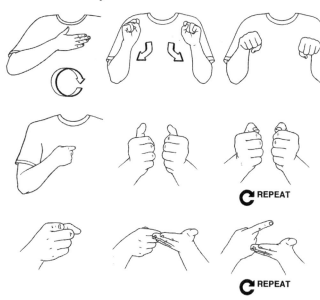

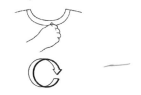

Sorry...

that's fucking ridiculous.

that train left the station and blew up.

This means that the conversation's moved on and we ain't going back. It's usually used in group conversation when you missed something but no one wants to repeat it.

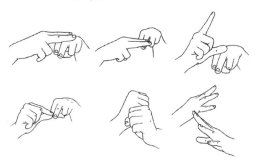

that's over my head.

·····Get me out of here

'Scuse me.

My bad.

Bye.

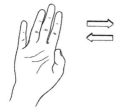

Peace out.

I'm gonna roll. ; I'm gonna take off.

ILY

Literally, "I love you"; friendly sign for goodbye.

See you later.

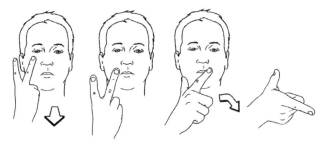

CHAPTER 2

FRIENDLY
SIGN LANGUAGE

You wanna make deaf friends? Well the most important thing is to learn sign! Sure you could rely on gestures and body language or type it up on the phone or even write it down on paper like an old timer. But after a nanosecond, these methods become so tiresome and slow, you might as well be chiseling it out in stone. If you don't put some effort into learning some sign, or finger spelling at least, that deafie is gonna lose interest in trying to talk to you so there goes your chance at a friend or more.

•••••Friends

My girls

My boys

BFF

Classmate

Roomie

REPEAT

Coworker

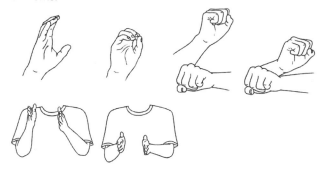

·····Lovers and flings

Oh, him/her? That's just my...

girlfriend.

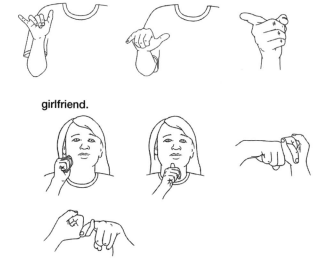

boyfriend.

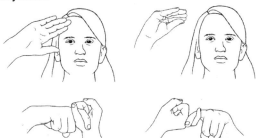

fiancé.

wife.

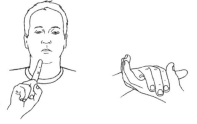

husband.

sweetheart.
Hands over heart.

friend with benefits.

  HAND AT HIP

fuck buddy.

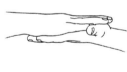

lover.

•••••Characters

He/She is a total…

loser.

snob.

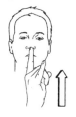 

slacker.

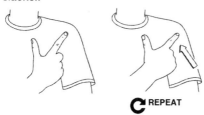

↻ REPEAT

nerd.

hipster.
Move shoulders back and forth.

jock.

flirt.

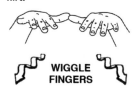

WIGGLE FINGERS

genius.

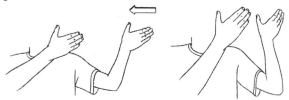

hippie.

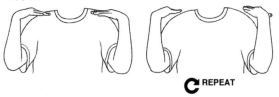

REPEAT

dipshit.

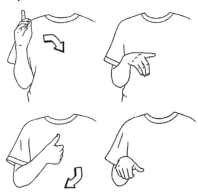

party pooper.

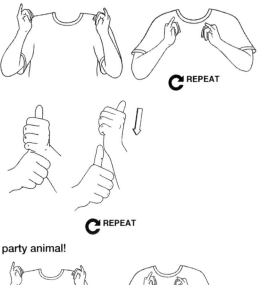

party animal!

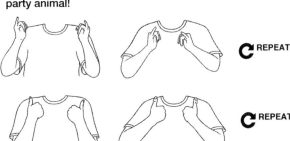

·····All in the family

That's my…

ma.

sis.

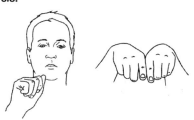

bro.

CHAPTER 3

PARTY
SIGN LANGUAGE

Ain't no party like … a deaf kid's party? Ever wonder what your local deafies are doing on Saturday night? Well, it's not much different from anyone else who likes to have a good time. A deaf bash runs the spectrum from your average house kegger infused with beer-pong, flip-cup and beer-bongs to a night out at the local bar or club to get boozed. The only difference tends to be lighting. While the hearing population may struggle to hold a conversation in a crowded, thumping club, deaf bar-hoppers have the same problem in darkened watering holes—making a decently lit bar an immediate favorite.

Now, you may think that deaf events are awkwardly quiet—but you're dead wrong. More than three quarters of the deaf parties we've ever been to have ended up with the cops having to shut it down for noise violations. Mix alcohol with a bunch of festive and flirty deaf people (with no volume control), and you might as well be at a raucous rock concert.

·····Let's party!

Let's hit up that...

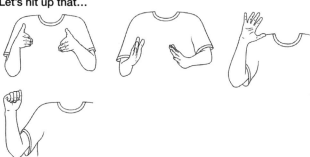

club.

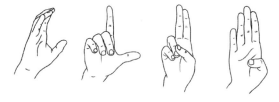

house party.

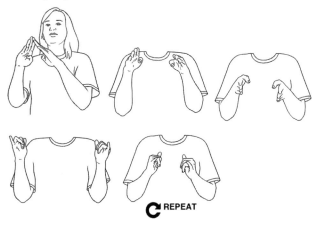

dive bar.

seedy alley.

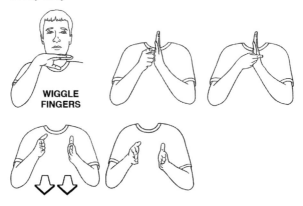

WIGGLE FINGERS

happy hour!

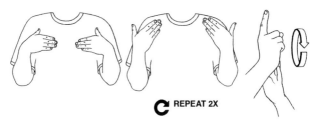

REPEAT 2X

truck stop.

REPEAT

This place is bumpin'!

REPEAT

Check out the hotties!

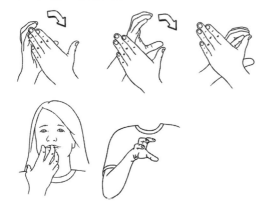

What a shithole!

REPEAT

Are you up for…

an all-nighter?

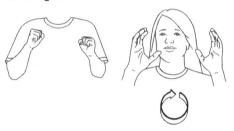

getting drunk?

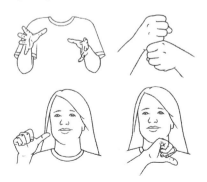

beer pong?

C REPEAT

Want to come back to my place?

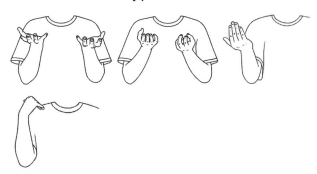

·····Booze

Gimme a…

brewskie.

whiskey.

REPEAT

vodka.

 REPEAT

tequila.

REPEAT

mixed drink.

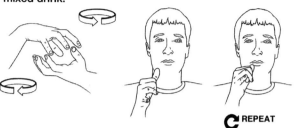

↻ REPEAT

margarita.

shot.

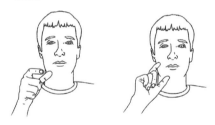

·····Getting high

Slurring your words when drunk or stoned is a universal occurrence—even in sign language. Don't be surprised if your hands don't want to say what your brain is thinking or if you lose track of what you're talking about when you have to use your hands to stop yourself from face-planting on the ground. Some deaf people will switch from Signed Exact English to American Sign Language—which is kind of like hearing someone with perfect grammar start saying sentences backward.

Got any…?

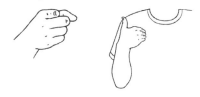

Where can I get some…?

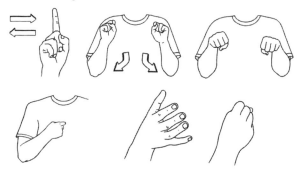

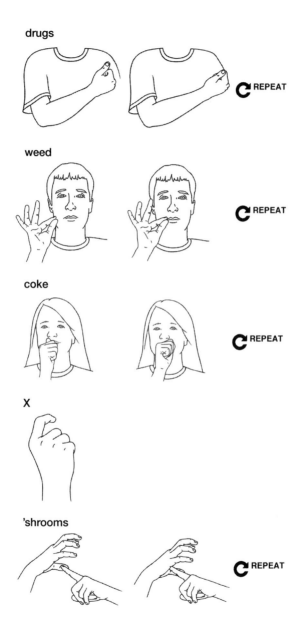

drugs

REPEAT

weed

REPEAT

coke

REPEAT

X

'shrooms

REPEAT

I'm wasted!

I'm hungover.

I need to puke.

He/She just passed out!

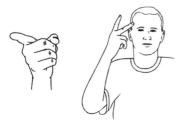

CHAPTER 4

BODY
SIGN LANGUAGE

If you wanna survive in deaf culture, pay attention to your body language. Trying to compliment someone? Be sure you make and keep eye contact otherwise they may not even know you are talking to them and your best line is missed. Also smile (you're being friendly right?) and nod to show you appreciate what you're complimenting. On the other hand, if you're talking shit about someone and you don't want them to see, turn your back to shield what your signing and use smaller gestures—the sign version of whispering. Keep in mind if you don't want to get caught, don't point or make eye contact with the person your are talking about!

You have such...

pretty eyes.

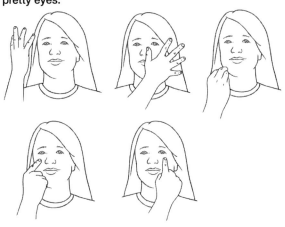

a hot bod.

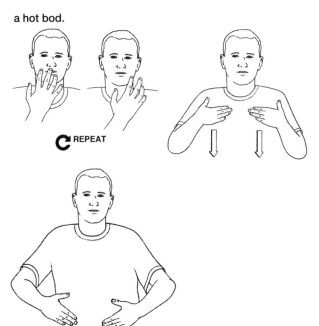

REPEAT

a nice face.

a huge rack.

a beer belly.

a fugly face.

a cute ass.

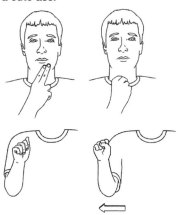

a fat ass.

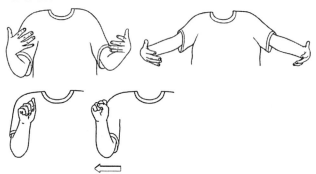

He/She is…

cute.

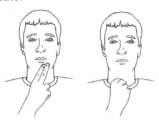

beautiful.

really hairy.

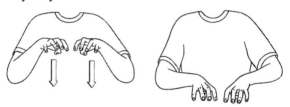

sexy.

skinny.

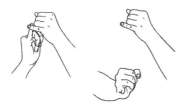

fine.

stylish.

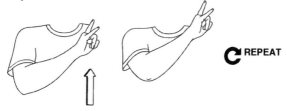

REPEAT

chunky.

REPEAT

•••••Bodily functions

I just...

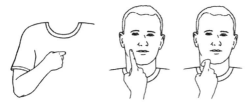

pissed. (rude one only)

↻ REPEAT

took a nasty shit.

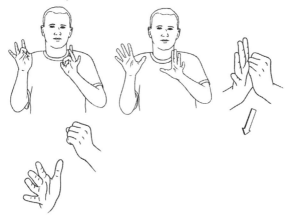

ripped a horrendous fart.

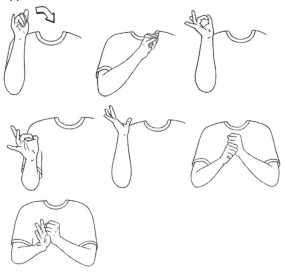

puked.

·····Getting sick

I feel sick.

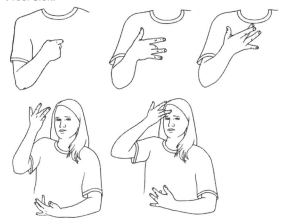

I have…

the runs/squirts.

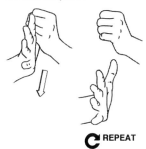

REPEAT

constipation.

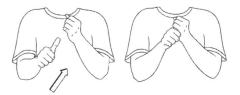

a headache.

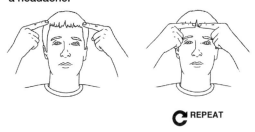

REPEAT

my period.

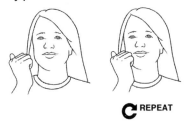

REPEAT

a stomach ache.

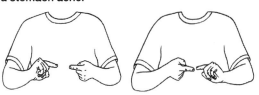

to go to the bathroom.

REPEAT

I feel like crap.

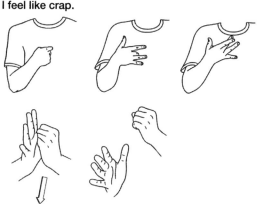

CHAPTER 5

HORNY SIGN LANGUAGE

Congratulations! You've just met some seriously smokin' deafie at the bar and, using your dirty new signs, things are going smashingly well. We're happy to take all the credit. Unfortunately, you've gotten to the point where it's time to make your move and take this hottie home. Feeling a little nervous? You're probably wondering if your regular moves and foreplay are going to cross the language barrier. Not to worry, we've got you covered.

First off, flirting and talking dirty is incredibly fun in sign language— you can do right in public and nobody catches a thing. Sure, you might make your soon-to-be partner blush, but those nasty things you're saying are for their eyes only.

Once you're alone and things are getting hot, feel free let your hands go silent and focus on more important things. Facial expressions and body language are the key to good foreplay when your hands are occupied and you can't be heard, so pay attention and save your lingual dexterity for the fun stuff.

·····Fucking

I wanna …

Let's go to your place and…

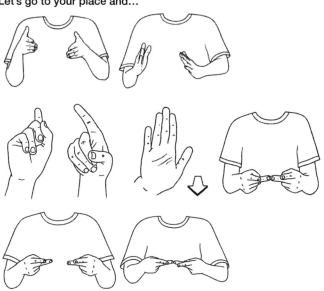

fuck.

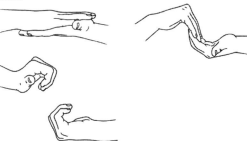

have a quickie.

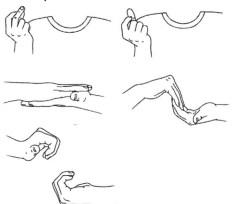

make a twin sandwich.

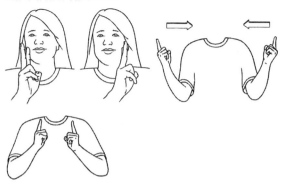

tossed salad.

WIGGLE TONGUE

dry hump.

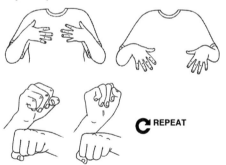

REPEAT

I'm horny.

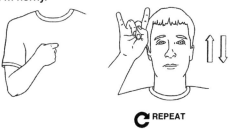

REPEAT

I'd like to bone her.

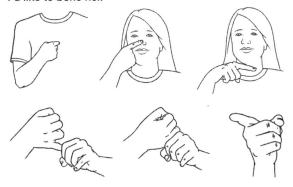

VOLUME CONTROL: DO YOU HAVE IT?)))

Being deaf and not knowing how much sound you're making can lead to some fun situations. What happens when your deaf girlfriend has both a very easy-to-understand speaking voice and an insatiable sexual appetite? Pure, unadulterated awkwardness. In crowds, brace yourself for the occasional, "I want your cock," in front of a vacationing family, or the shouted "You wanna have a threesome?" while your mother is in the next room. Then there's the bedroom, where the guttural grunts and shrieking moans of love making tend to have the volume turned way the fuck up. Don't blush if you try to sneak in a quickie only to have a rousing round of applause from the partygoers in the next room. Hope you don't embarrass too easily.

·····Positions

I wanna…

Let's do it…

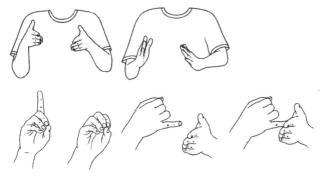

missionary.

doggy style.

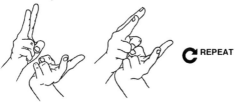

cowgirl.

reverse cowgirl.

anal.

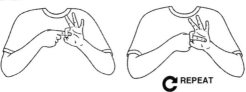

rough.

with people watching.

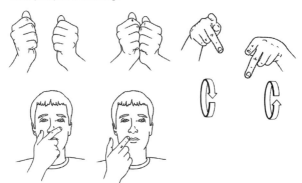

Blow job

REPEAT

Cunnilingus

WIGGLE TONGUE

Suck my tits.

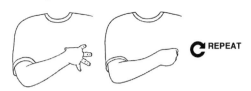

⟳ REPEAT

•••••Feeling adventurous?

I'd like to try…

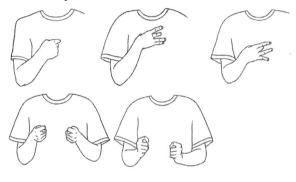

stripping.

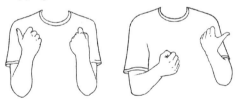

a vibrator.

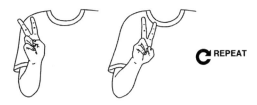

C REPEAT

69 (gay).

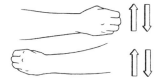

69 (lesbian).

WIGGLE MIDDLE FINGERS

69 (hetero).

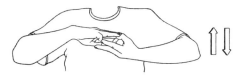

69 (hetero).

Because one isn't enough.

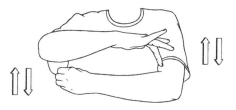

a threesome.

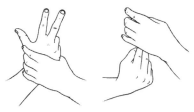

an orgy.

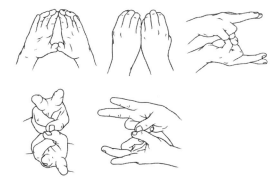

two in the pink one in the stink.

REPEAT

Don't be nervous.

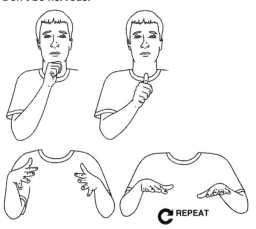

REPEAT

Bite me.

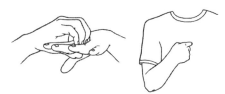

I'm your slave, you're my master.

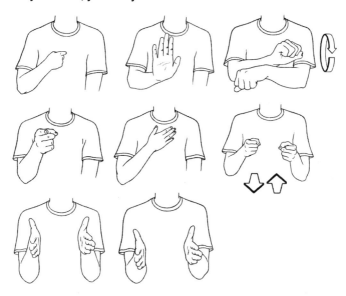

Get on your knees and smile like a donut.

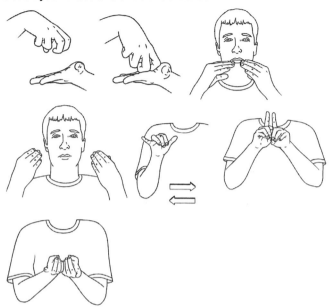

•••••Genitalia

Touch my dick.

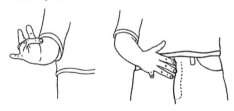

I'd like to touch your...

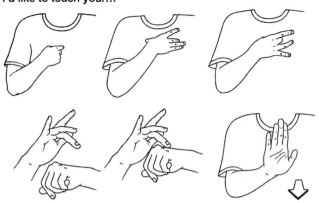

You've got (a) great...

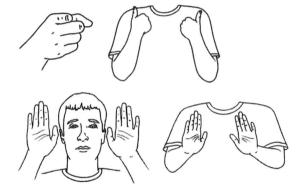

I fucking love your…

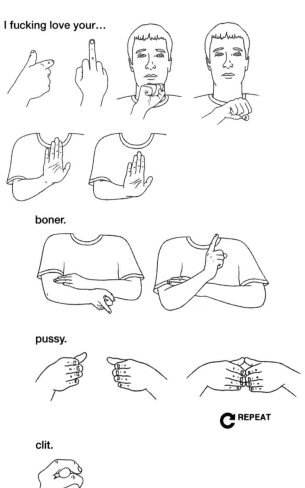

boner.

pussy.

 REPEAT

clit.

ass.

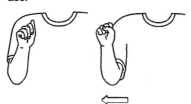

asshole.

tits.

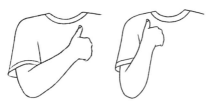

I'm hung like a horse.

·····I'm coming!

I'm getting...

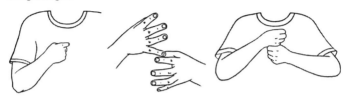

hard.

wet.

I'm going to…

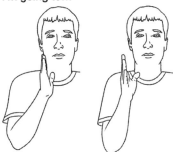

I just…

orgasmed/came.

This hurts.

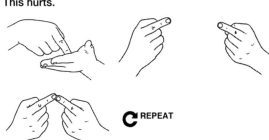

REPEAT

This feels amazing!

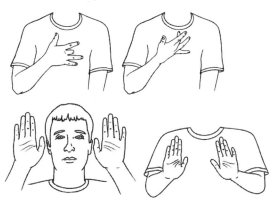

Fuck me harder!

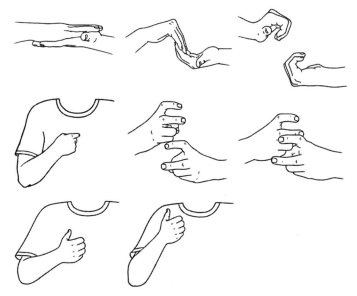

Well, that was crappy.

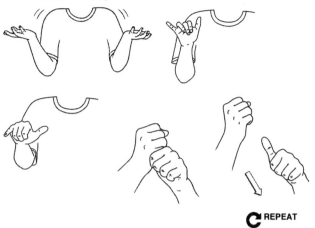

REPEAT

·····Masturbation

I think I'm just gonna stay in and...

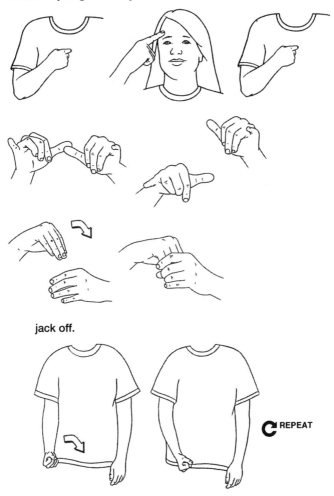

jack off.

C REPEAT

choke the chicken.

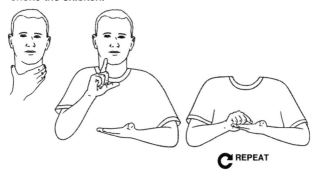

REPEAT

play with my vibrator.

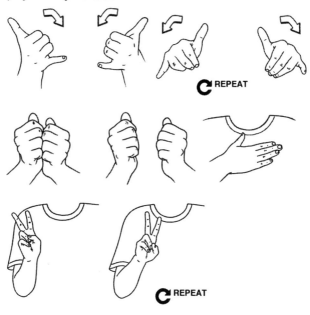

REPEAT

REPEAT

·····Sex industry

Sex shop

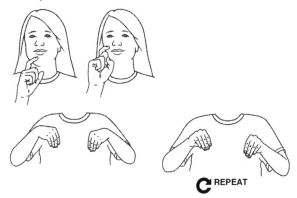

Stripper/strip club

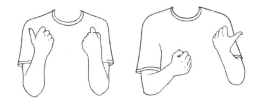

Prostitute/hooker

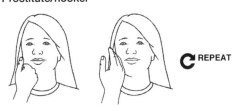

CHAPTER 6

ANGRY SIGN LANGUAGE

Understanding body language is important when it comes to friendly conversation and sexual attraction, but it can also save your ass. When deaf people get angry, they tend to sign much faster than normal—with more dramatic and exaggerated hand signs—so, if two deafies are signing at each other too fast for you to understand, you might want to check out their body language and facial expressions and get out of the way if they look mad cuz some shit is about to go down.

·····Light insults

You're a stupid...

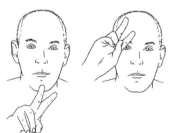

moron.

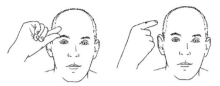

dumbass.

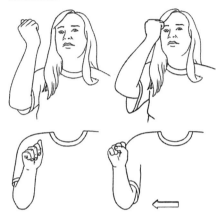

sick fuck.

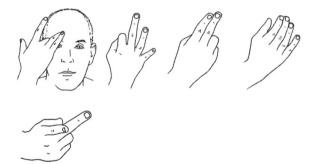

We fuck. (dislike each other)

What's the matta with ya?

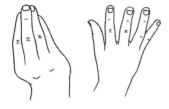

I'm getting pissed, dude.

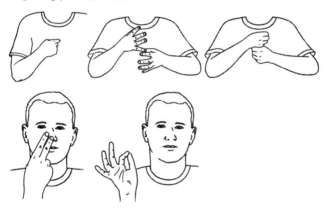

What the fuck is your problem?

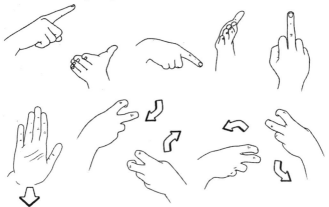

•••••Bullshit by the pound

I've had enough of your bullshit. (three different signs)

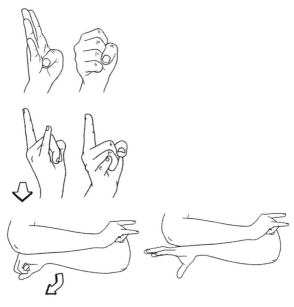

·····Talking shit

You just fucked with the wrong person...

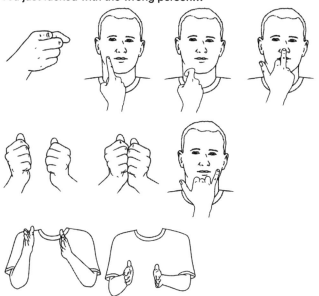

Chill...

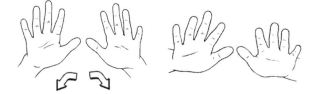

bitch.

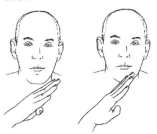

asshole.

dumbfuck.

motherfucker.

cunt.

Fuck off!

 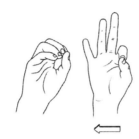

Fuck you!

Don't fuck with me.

Don't give a fuck.

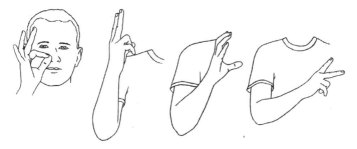

Ima fuck you up so bad.

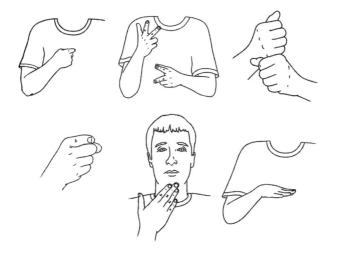

····Let's get ready to rumble

Enemy

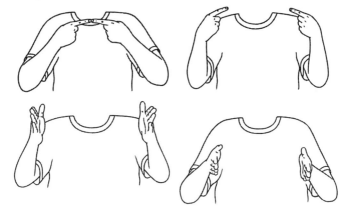

Fighting

C REPEAT

I'm gonna whoop ass.

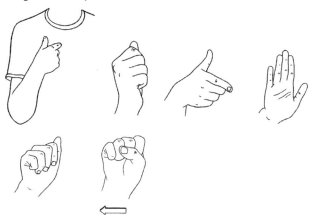

Dude just got...

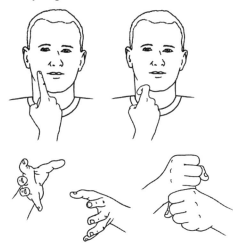

punched.

choked.

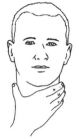

blood everywhere.

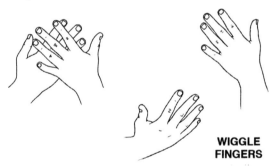

**WIGGLE
FINGERS**

You just gave that asshole…

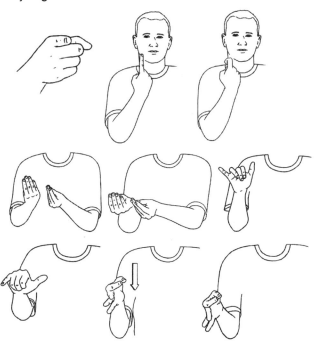

a broken bone.

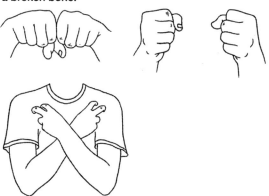

·····Stopping a fight

The cops are coming.

Calm the fuck down.

↻ REPEAT

Pow
This is what you say to someone when you've won an argument.

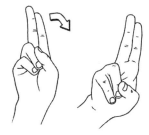

CHAPTER 7

SPORTY SIGN LANGUAGE

You might think that a deaf person playing sports may look uncoordinated and like a lousy team player. That ain't true. If you're playing with a deaf teammate for the first time, chances are it's going to make *you* look like an idiot when you repeatedly scream at your deaf forward to no avail. Instead, simply ask your teammate what hand gestures you should use to communicate on the field or court; after all, they've probably played a team sport before and know what they're doing.

Some kick-ass deafies have rocked the sports world, and knowing some of this trivia may help you break the ice at a party. Talking baseball? Just mention William "Dummy" Hoy who, among other things, set a major league record by throwing out three runners at home plate in one game, as well as hitting the first grand slam in the American League. Oh yeah, he also pretty much invented the catcher's "strike" sign—the most recognizable sign language in all of sports. It also never hurts to bring up Matt Hamill, a deaf wrestler (the real kind) and MMA fighter who's huge in deaf culture. If anyone still has doubts as to deaf people's abilities, just step into the ring with him.

Just remember this when you take the field: Playing with a deaf teammate may be frustrating at times, but it doesn't make them stupid. Thinking they are, however, makes you a dumbfuck.

·····Sports

Do you play…?

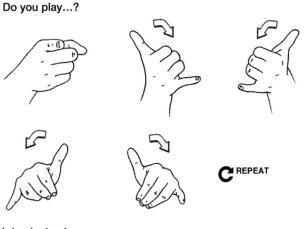

I dominate at…

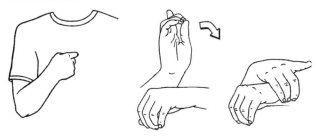

Let's watch the…game.

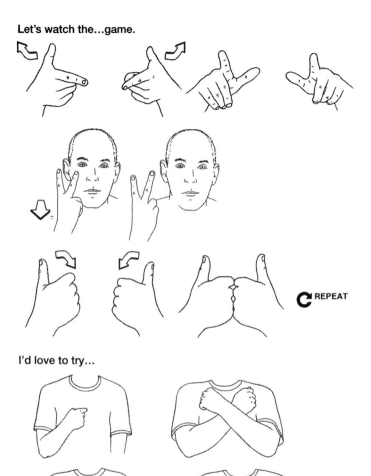

I'd love to try…

soccer

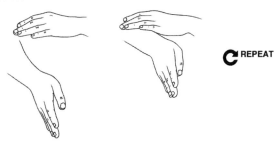

REPEAT

football

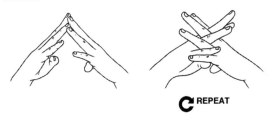

REPEAT

baseball

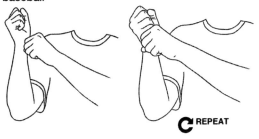

REPEAT

surfing

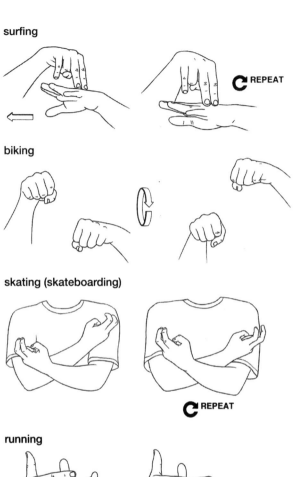

REPEAT

biking

skating (skateboarding)

REPEAT

running

REPEAT

swimming

REPEAT

hockey

REPEAT

tennis

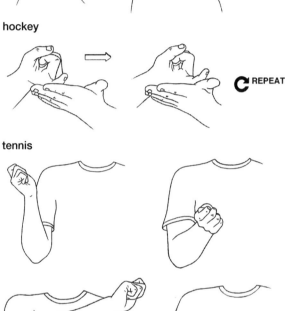

boxing

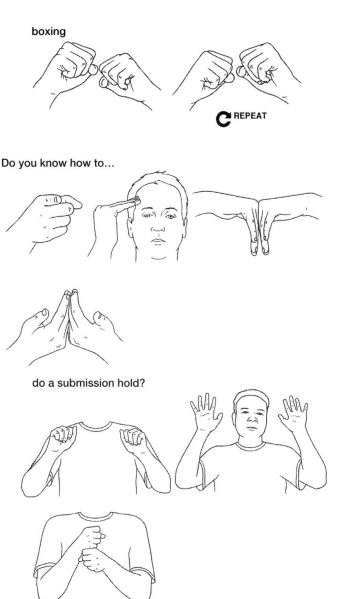

REPEAT

Do you know how to…

do a submission hold?

I will kick your ass at…

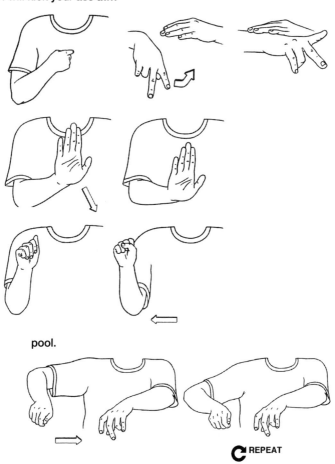

pool.

darts.

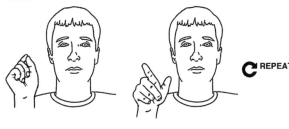

bowling.

·····Exercise

Let's hit the…

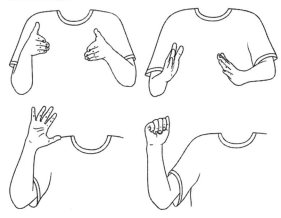

gym.

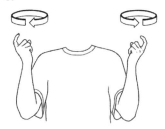

track.

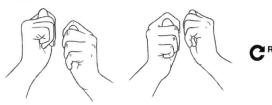

REPEAT

machines.

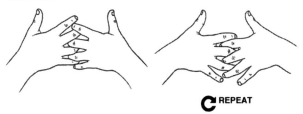

REPEAT

treadmill.

REPEAT

I want to work my…

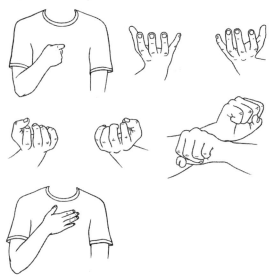

arms.

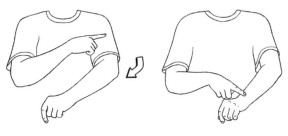

chest.

C REPEAT

Let's go for a run.

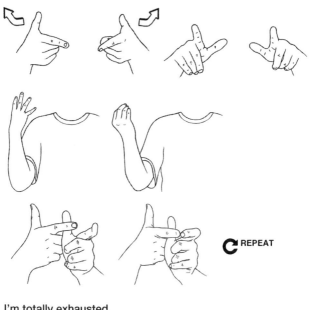

I'm totally exhausted.

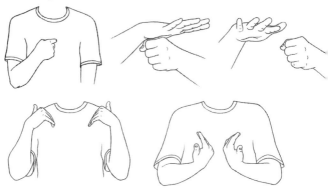

I'm sweating like a pig.

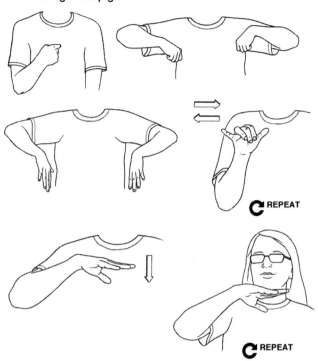

REPEAT

REPEAT

One more set!

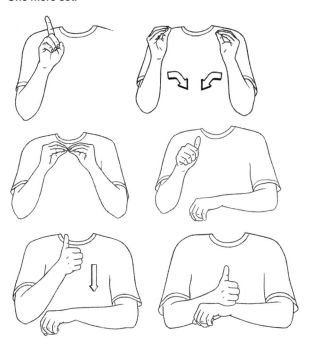

·····Other Ulysses Press Titles

Dirty Chinese: Everyday Slang from "What's Up?" to "F*%# Off!"
MATT COLEMAN & EDMUND BACKHOUSE, **$10.00**

Dirty Chinese includes phrases for every situation, even expressions to convince a local official that you have waited long enough and tipped him plenty already. A pronunciation guide and sample dialogues make this guide invaluable for those traveling to China.

Dirty French: Everyday Slang from "What's Up?" to "F*%# Off!"
ADRIEN CLAUTRIER & HENRY ROWE, **$10.00**

With this book, you can use sweet words to entice a local beauty into a walk along the Seine, and less-than-philosophical rebuffs for those zealous, espresso-fueled cafe "poets." There are enough insults and swear words to offend every person in France without even speaking to them in English.

Dirty German: Everyday Slang from "What's Up?" to "F*%# Off!"
DANIEL CHAFFEY, **$10.00**

Dirty German provides plenty of insults and swear words to piss off every person in Germany—without even mentioning that the Japanese make better cars—as well as explicit sex terms that'll even embarrass the women of Hamburg's infamous red light district.

Dirty Italian: Everyday Slang from "What's Up?" to "F*%# Off!"
GABRIELLE EUVINO, **$10.00**

This useful guide contains phrases for every situation, including insults to hurl at the refs during *fútbol* games. Readers learn sweet words to entice a local beauty into a romantic gondola ride, not-so-sweet remarks to ward off any overzealous Venetians, and more.

Dirty Japanese: Everyday Slang from "What's Up?" to "F*%# Off!"
MATT FARGO, **$10.00**

Even in traditionally minded Japan, slang from its edgy pop culture constantly enter into common usage. This book fills in the gap between how people really talk in Japan and what Japanese language students are taught.

Dirty Russian: Everyday Slang from "What's Up?" to "F*%# Off!"
ERIN COYNE & IGOR FISUN, **$10.00**

An invaluable guide for off-the-beaten-path travelers going to Russia, *Dirty Russian* is packed with enough insults and swear words to offend every person in Russia without even mentioning that they lost the Cold War.

Dirty Spanish: Everyday Slang from "What's Up?" to "F*%# Off!"
JUAN CABALLERO, **$10.00**

This handbook features slang for both Spain and Latin America. It includes a section on native banter that will help readers make friends over a pitcher of sangría and convince the local taco maker that it's OK to spice things up with a few fresh habaneros.

To order these books call 800-377-2542 or 510-601-8301, fax 510-601-8307, e-mail ulysses@ulyssespress.com, or write to Ulysses Press, P.O. Box 3440, Berkeley, CA 94703. All retail orders are shipped free of charge. California residents must include sales tax. Allow two to three weeks for delivery.

•••••About the Authors

While not a native at sign language, **Van James T** believes he learned to sign in the single-most fun way: dating. (If you don't have that option yet, this book hopes to give you the tools to put yourself out there and give it a try.) Van spent his early childhood living in Olympia, Washington; Isabel, Kansas; and Lawrence, Kansas. His family moved to the suburbs of Chicago when he was 9, and he's been in the area ever since. He resides in Naperville, Illinois, with his girlfriend, the inspiration for this book, who is deaf and responsible for his interest in the language.

Allison O grew up in a hearing family, but she and her half-identical twin were born deaf. Right after she was diagnosed at age two, she received hearing aids and began speech therapy. Because she knows how to read lips, she can communicate effectively using her voice, lip-reading, and signing. She has a bachelor's degree in social work and a master's degree in social work with a concentration in child welfare.

Both authors live in a spacious condo where Van continues to introduce Allison to dirty things that she shows him the signs for.